This book belongs to :

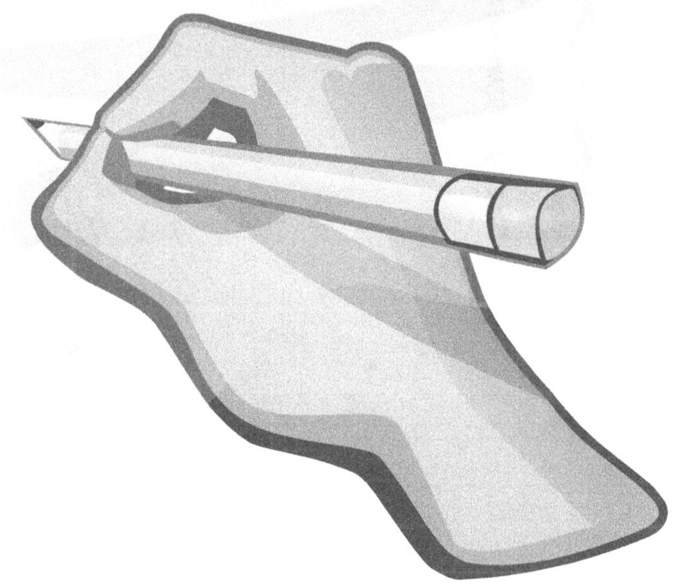

NUMBERS

1 2 3

1

ONE

2

TWO

3

THREE

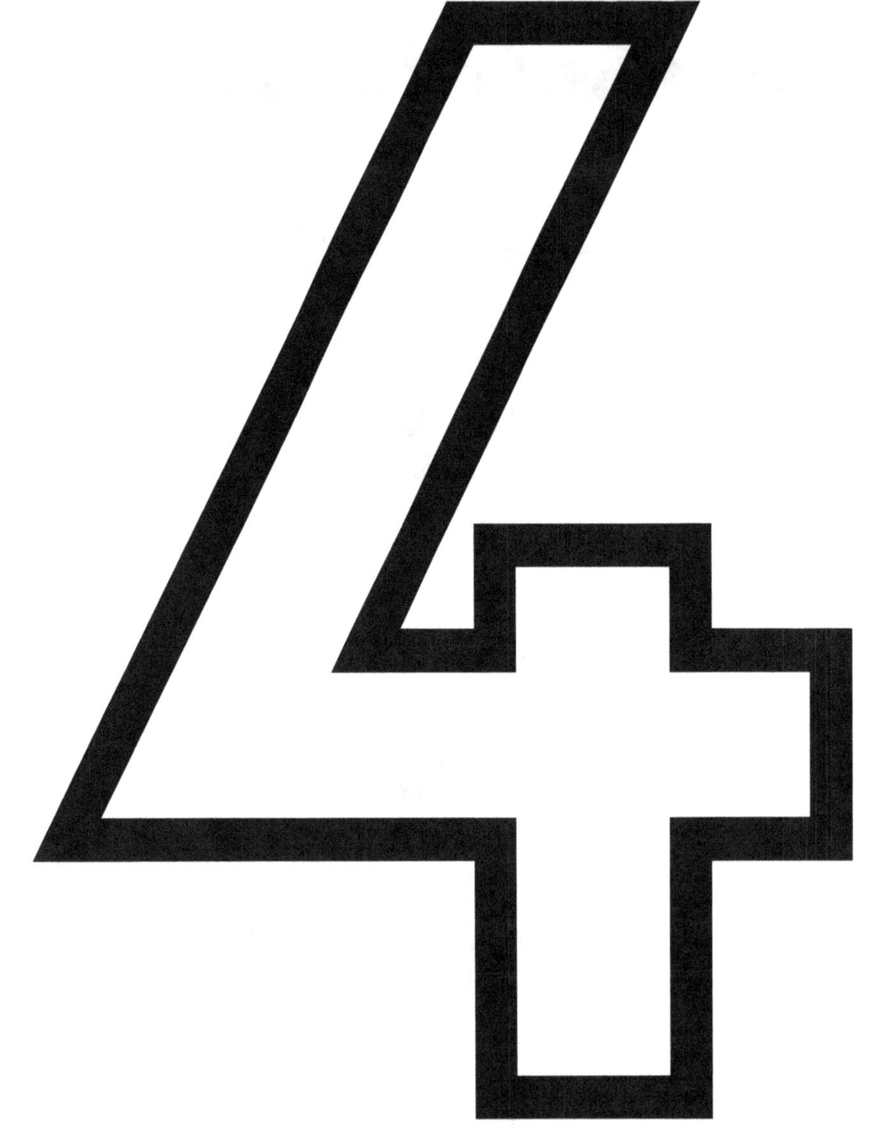

FOUR

5

FIVE

6

SIX

7

SEVEN

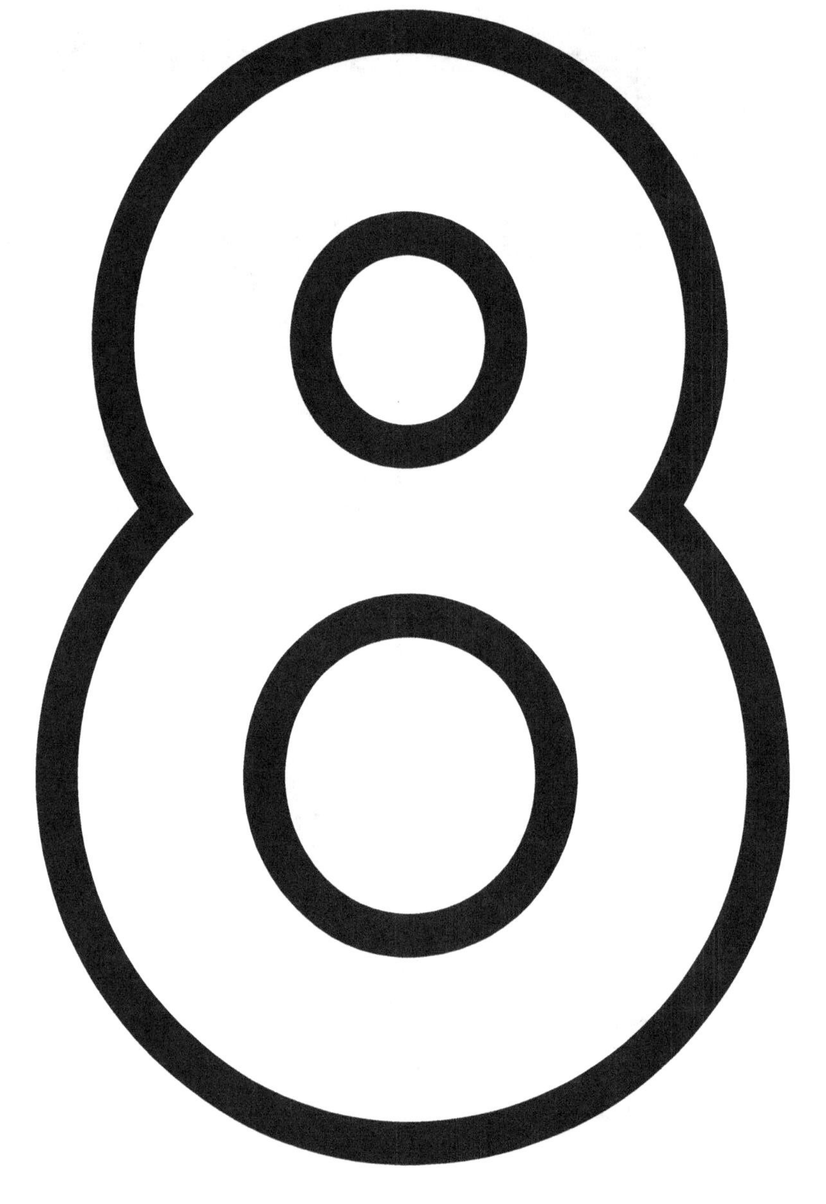

8
EIGHT

NINE

10

TEN

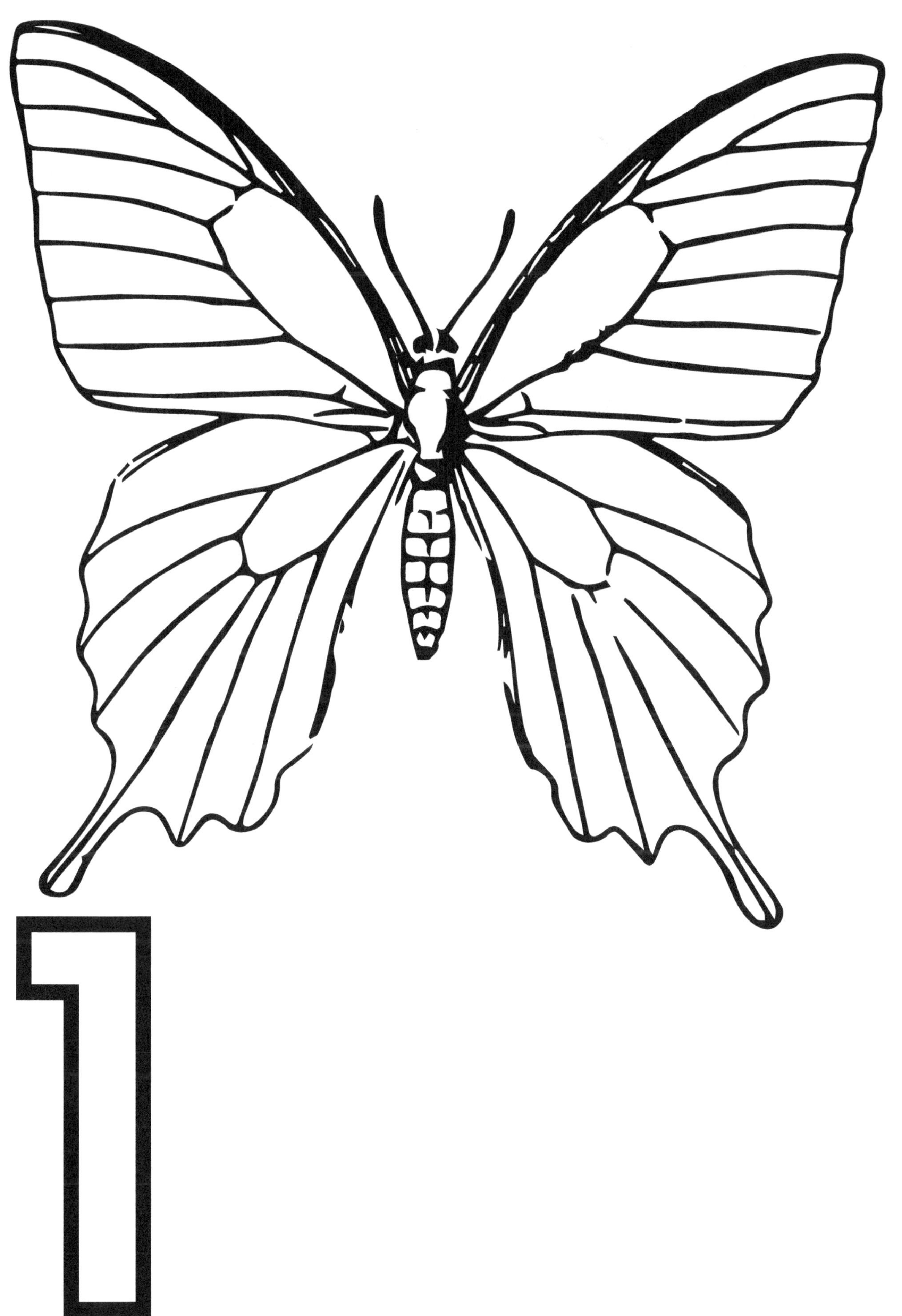

LETTERS

A

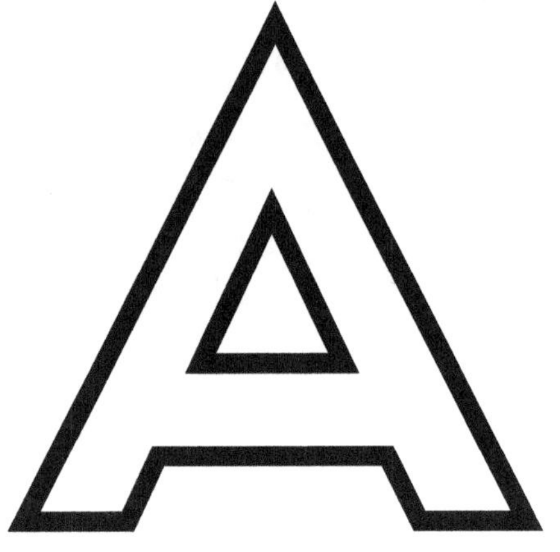

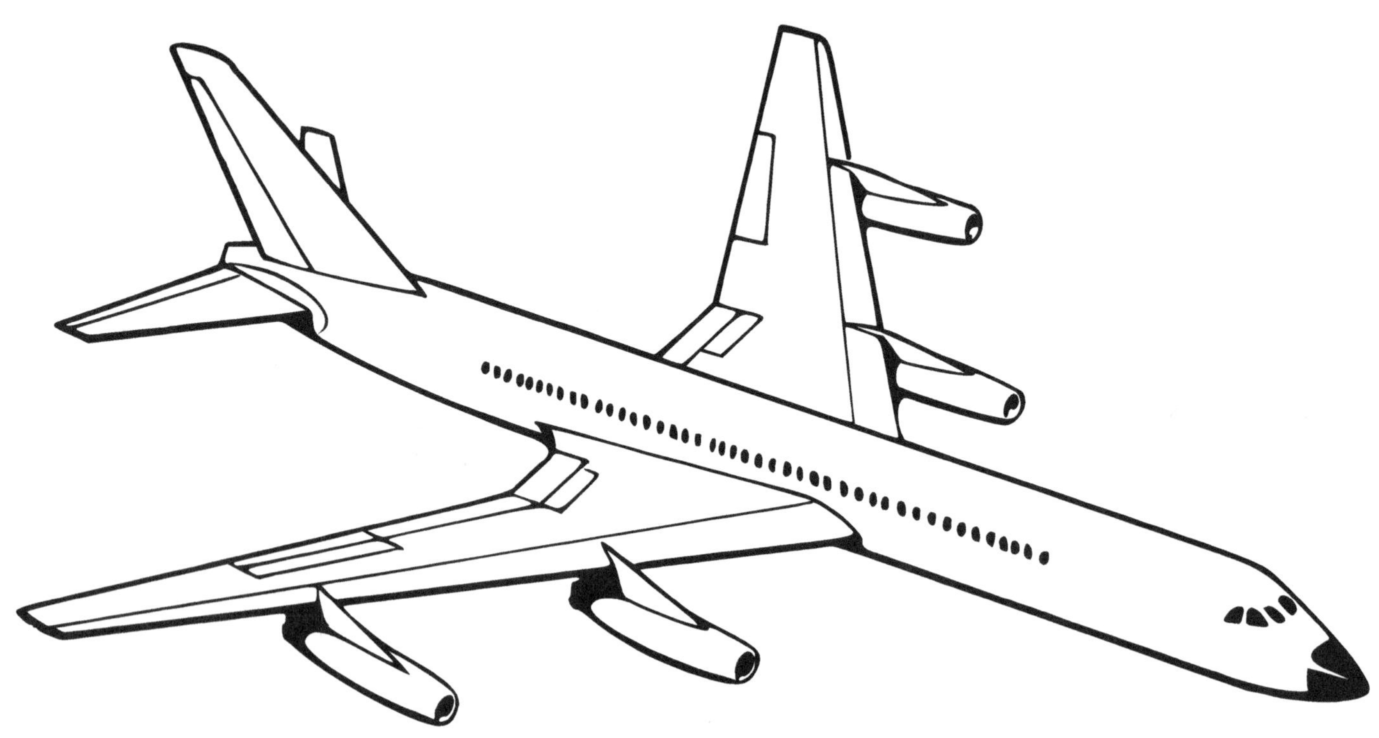

Airplane

B

Bicycle

C

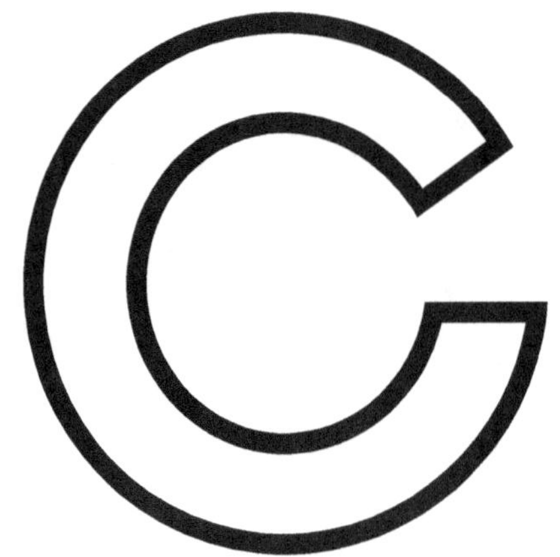

Car

D

Dog

E

Elephant

F

Flower

G

Girls

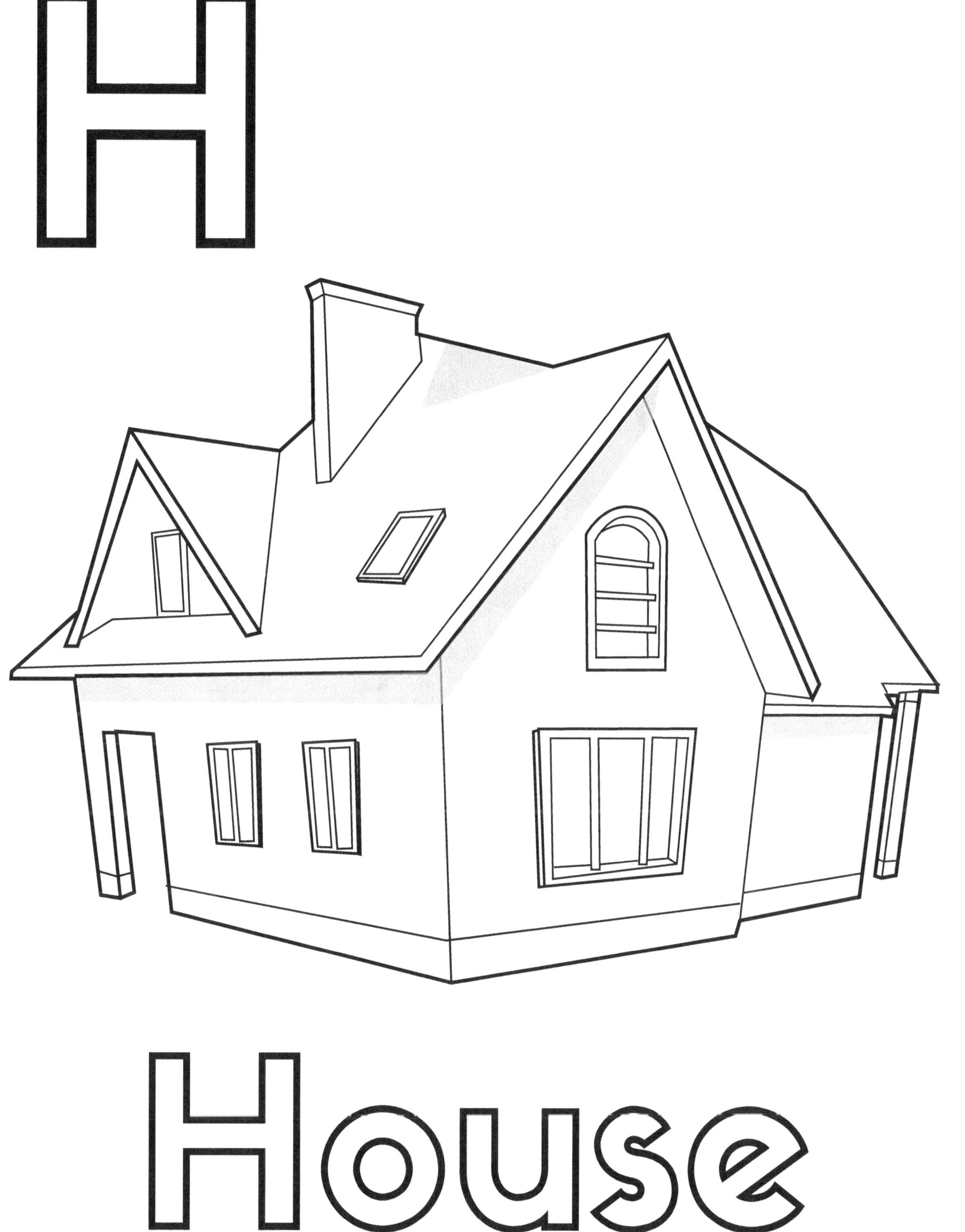

H
House

i

ice cream

J
Jacket

K

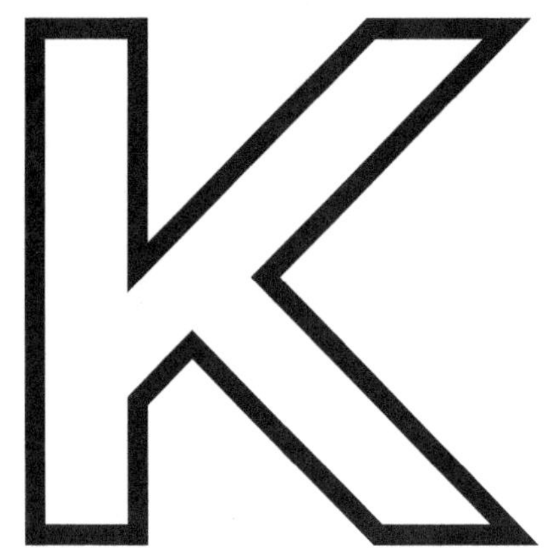

Key

L

Lemon

M

Mouse

N

Nurse

O
Octopus

P

Pig

Q

Quill

R
Rocket

S

Strawberry

T

Television

U

Umbrella

V

Vase

W
Whale

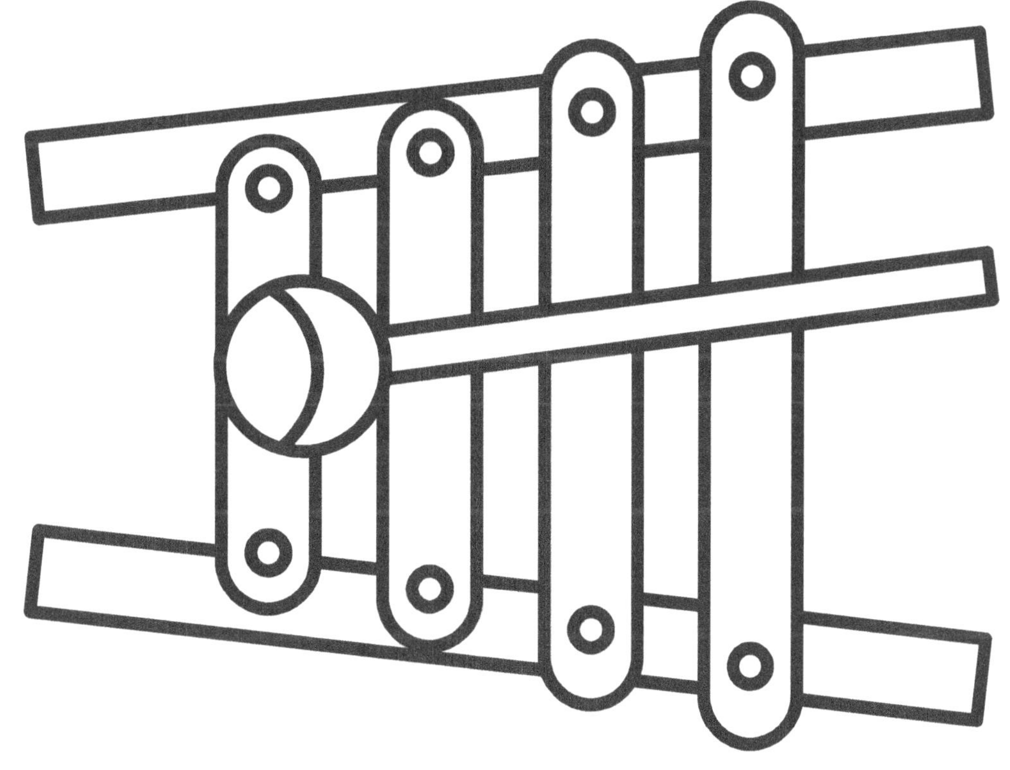

Xylophone

Y

Yogurt

Z

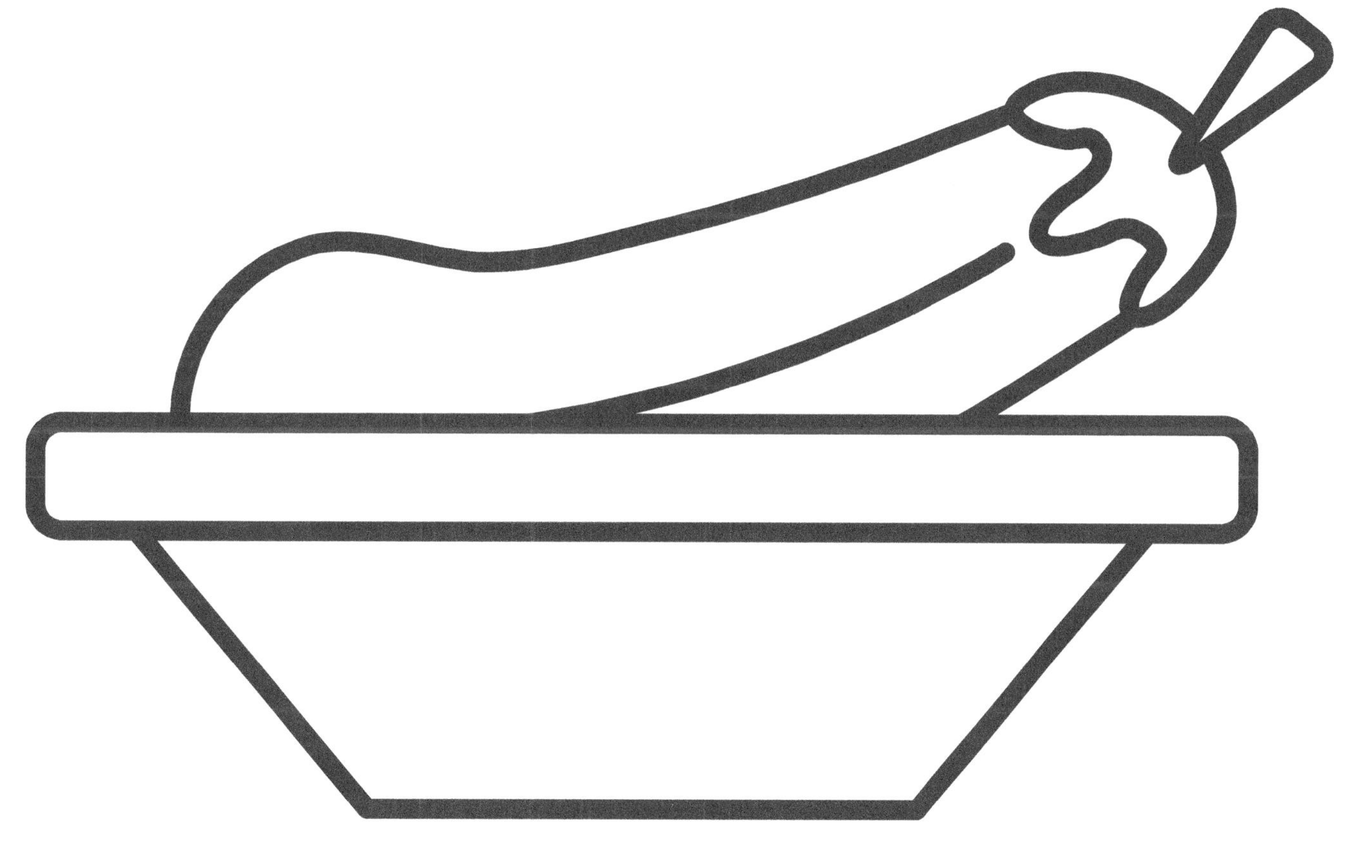

zucchini

SHAPES

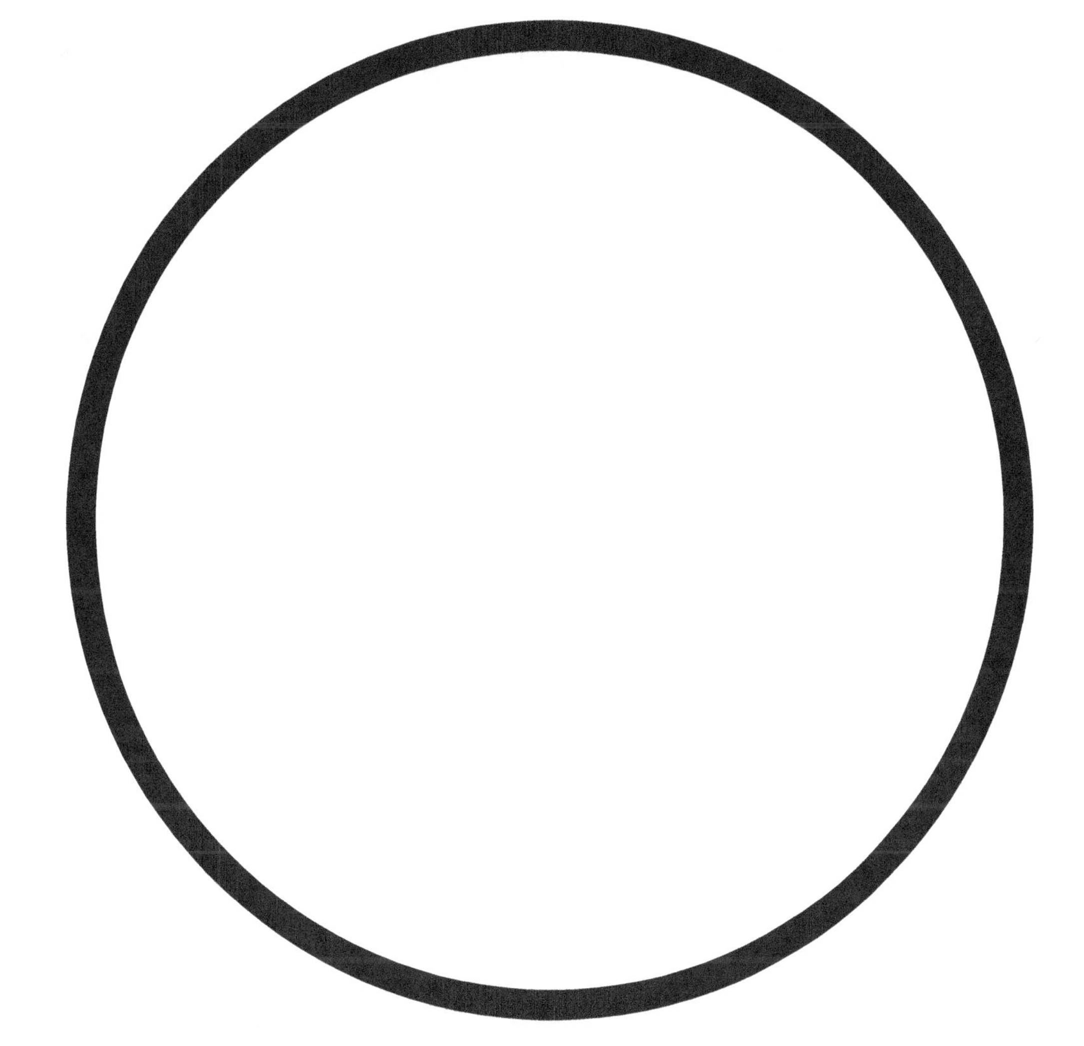

CIRCLE

SQUARE

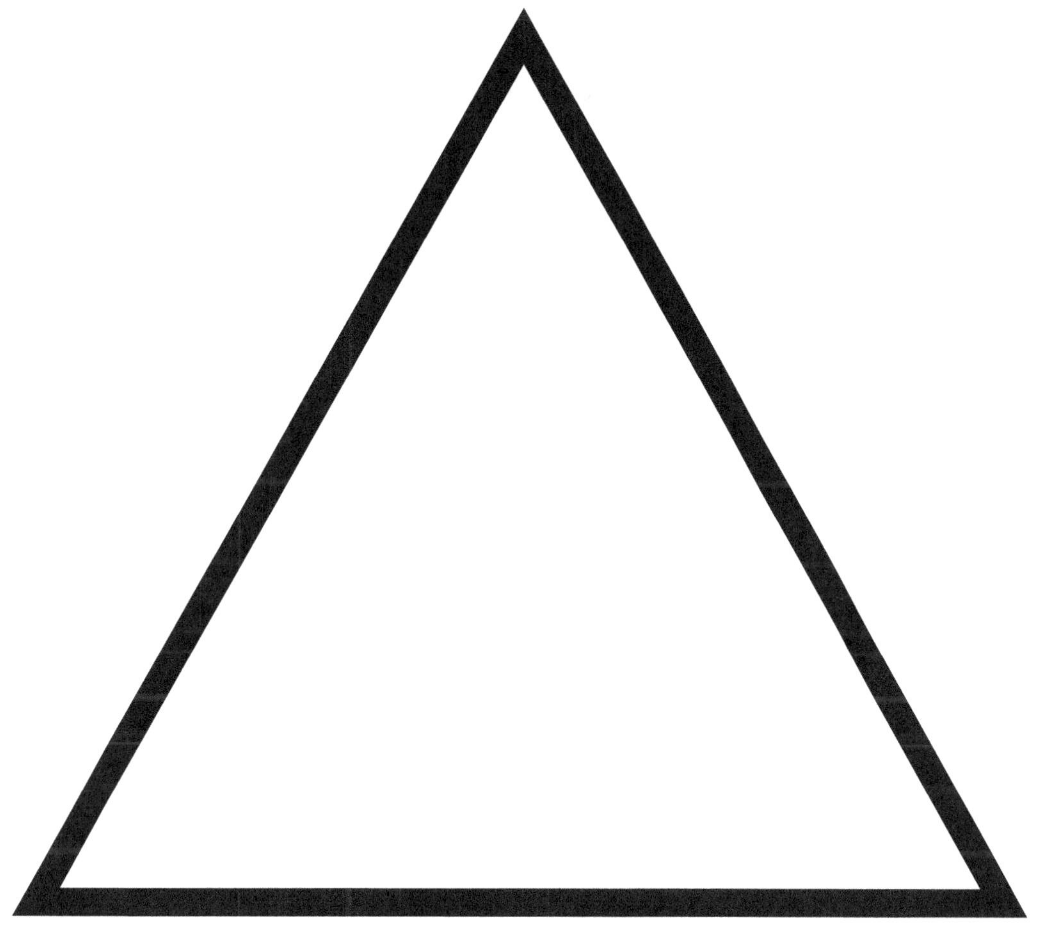

TRIANGLE

RECTANGLE

HEART

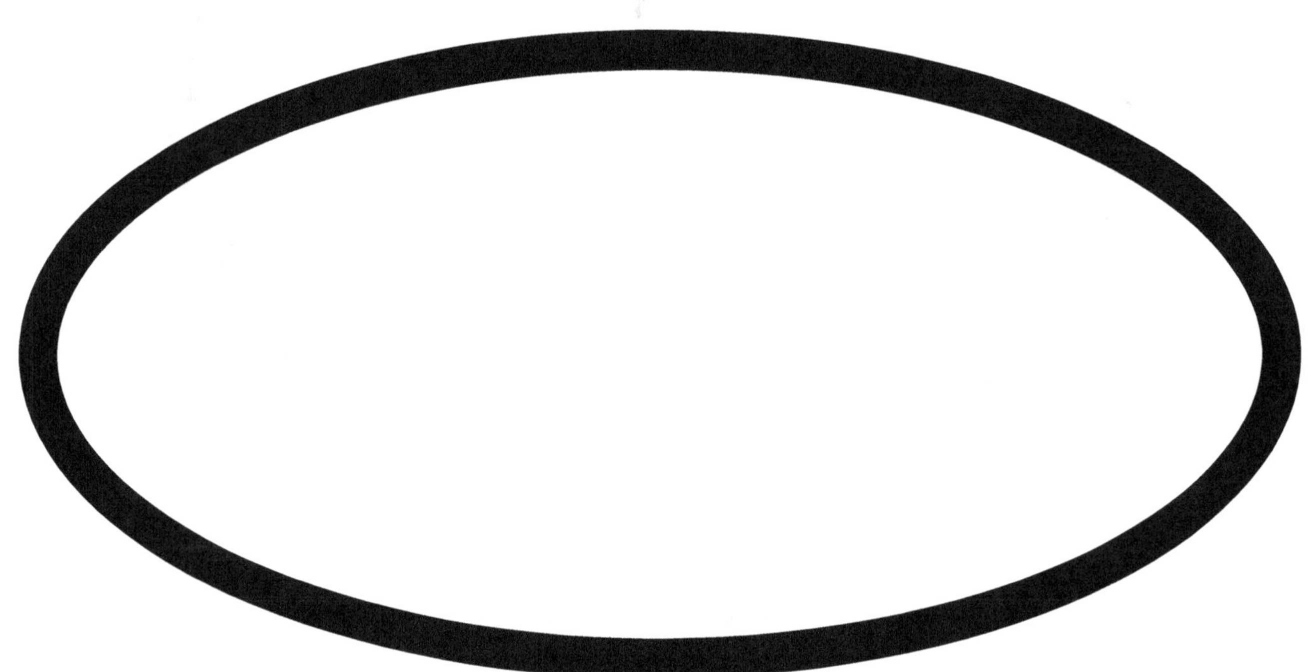

OVAL

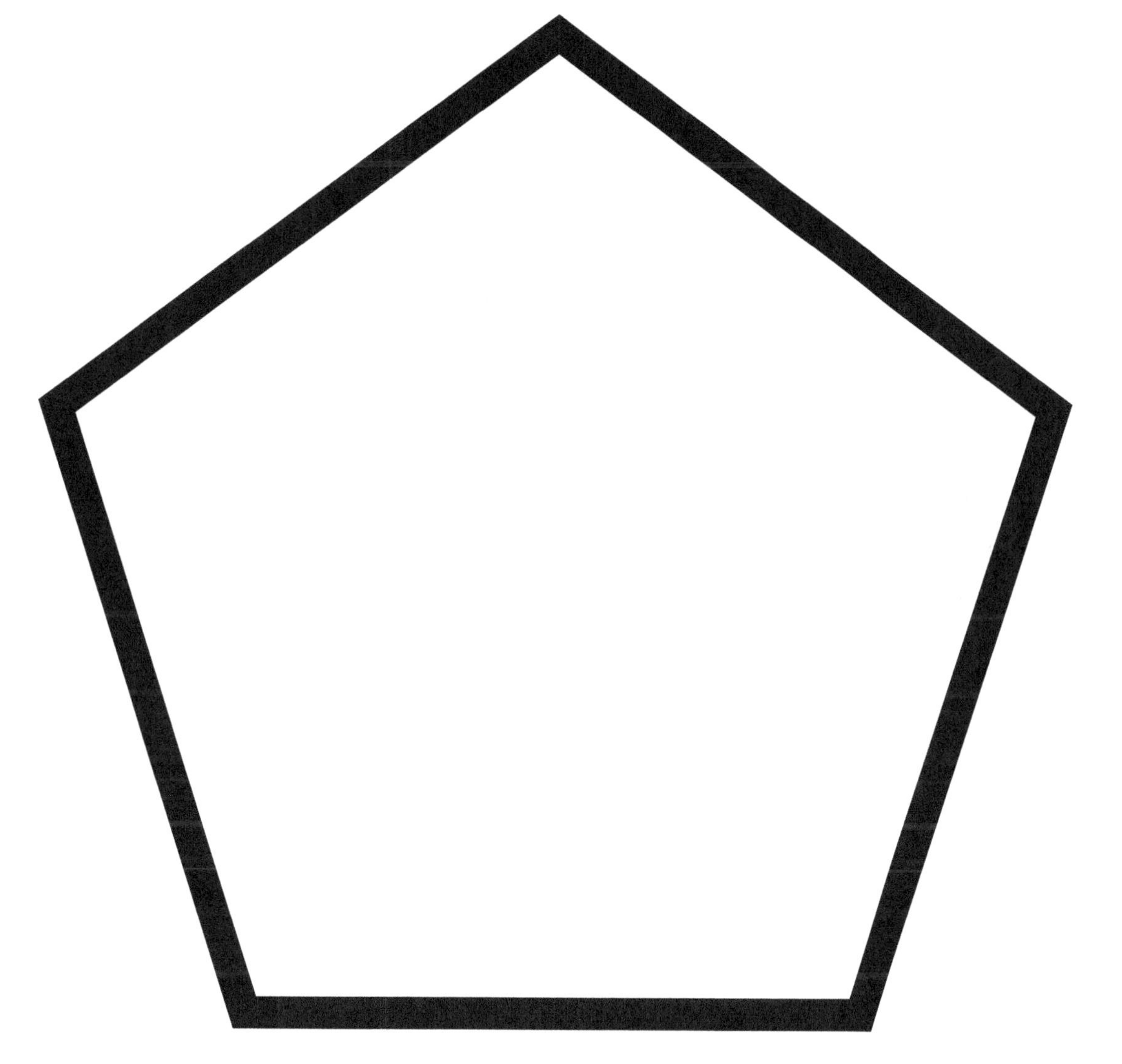

PENTAGON

STAR

COLORES

RED

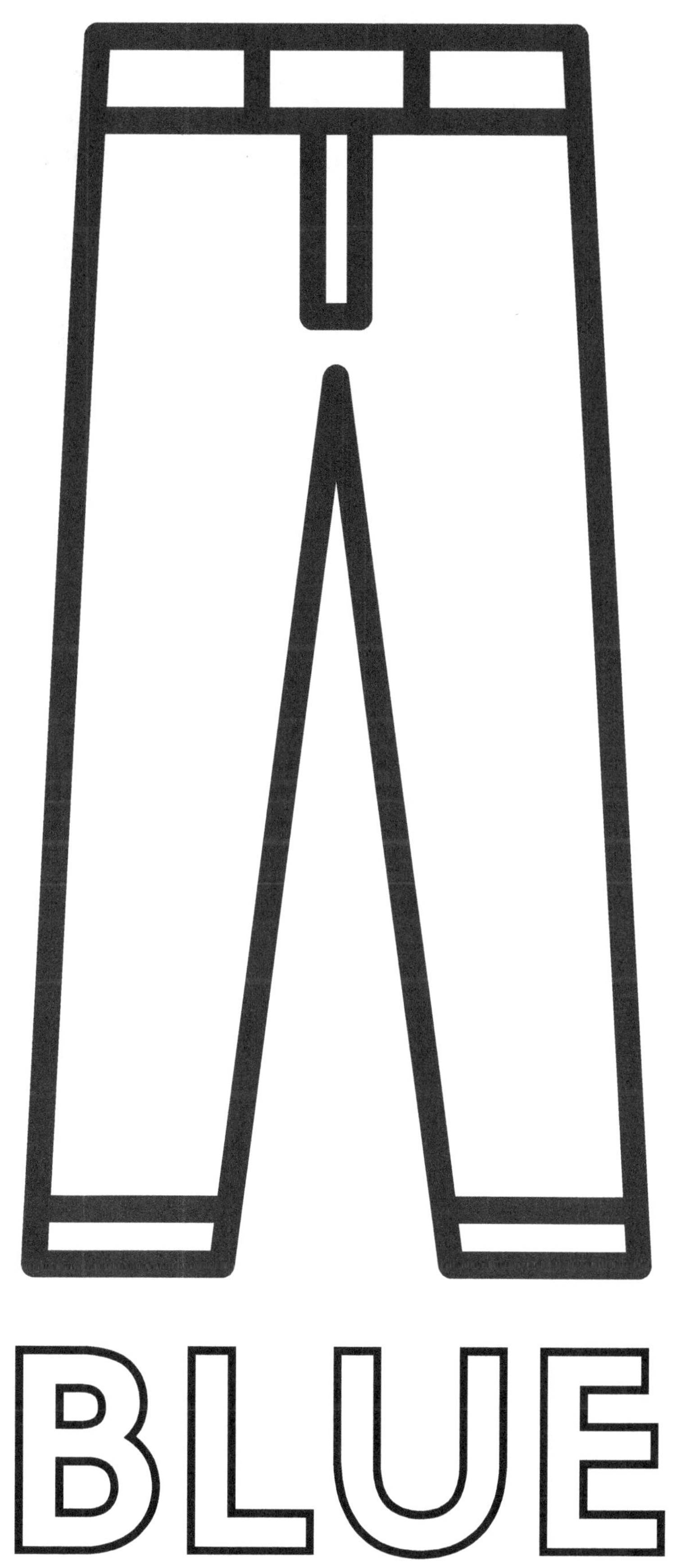

BLUE

YELLOW

PURPLE

GREEN

ORANGE

BLACK

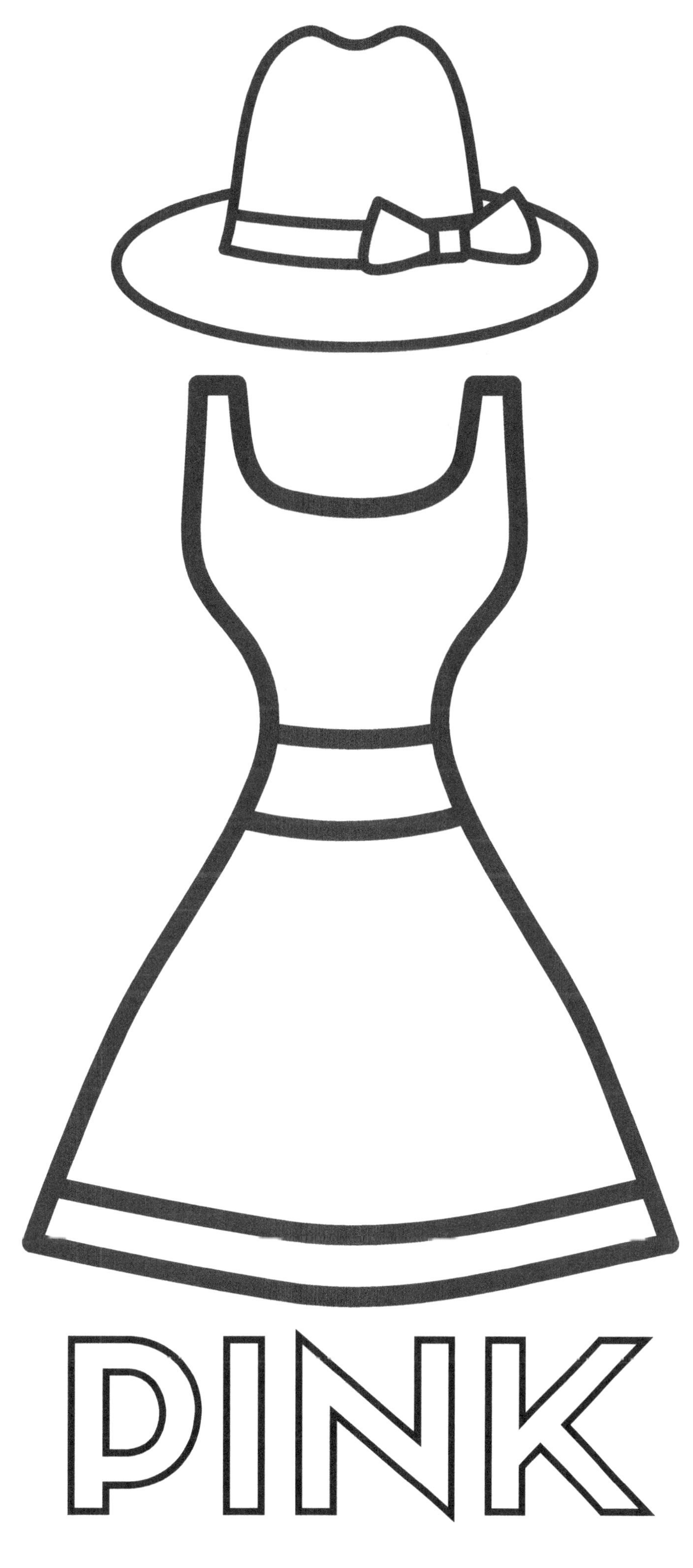
PINK

BROWN

GRAY

THINGS

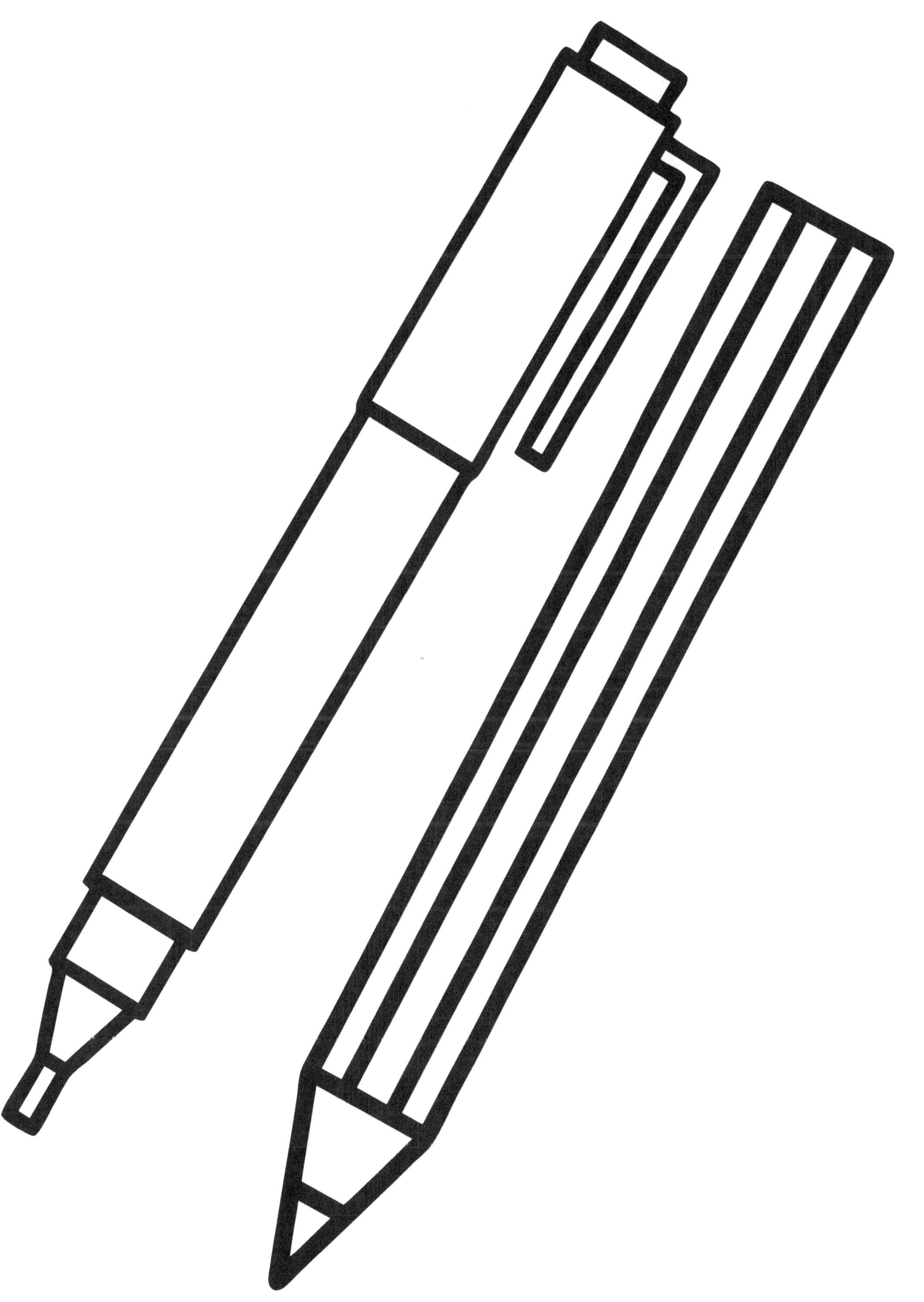

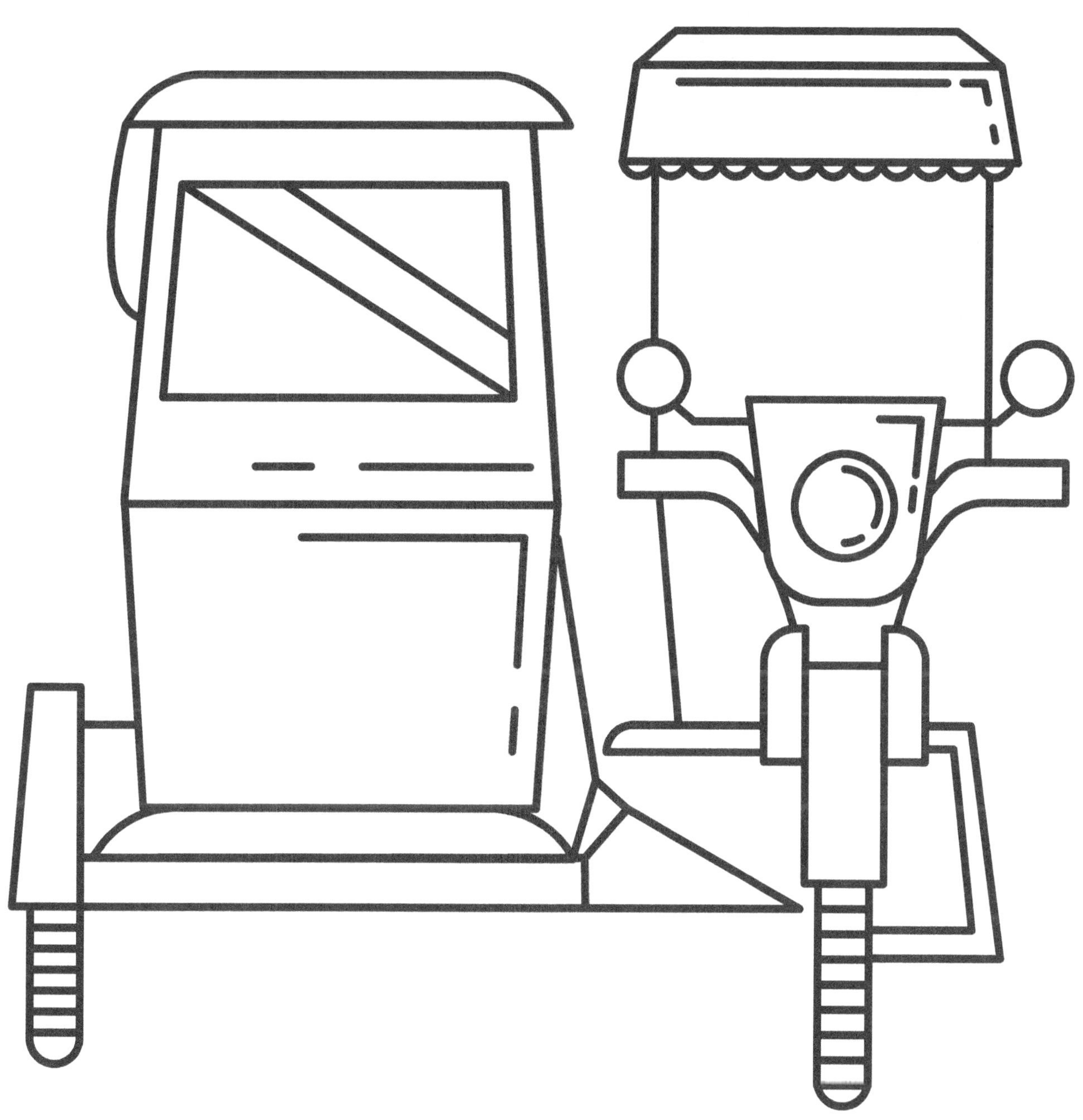

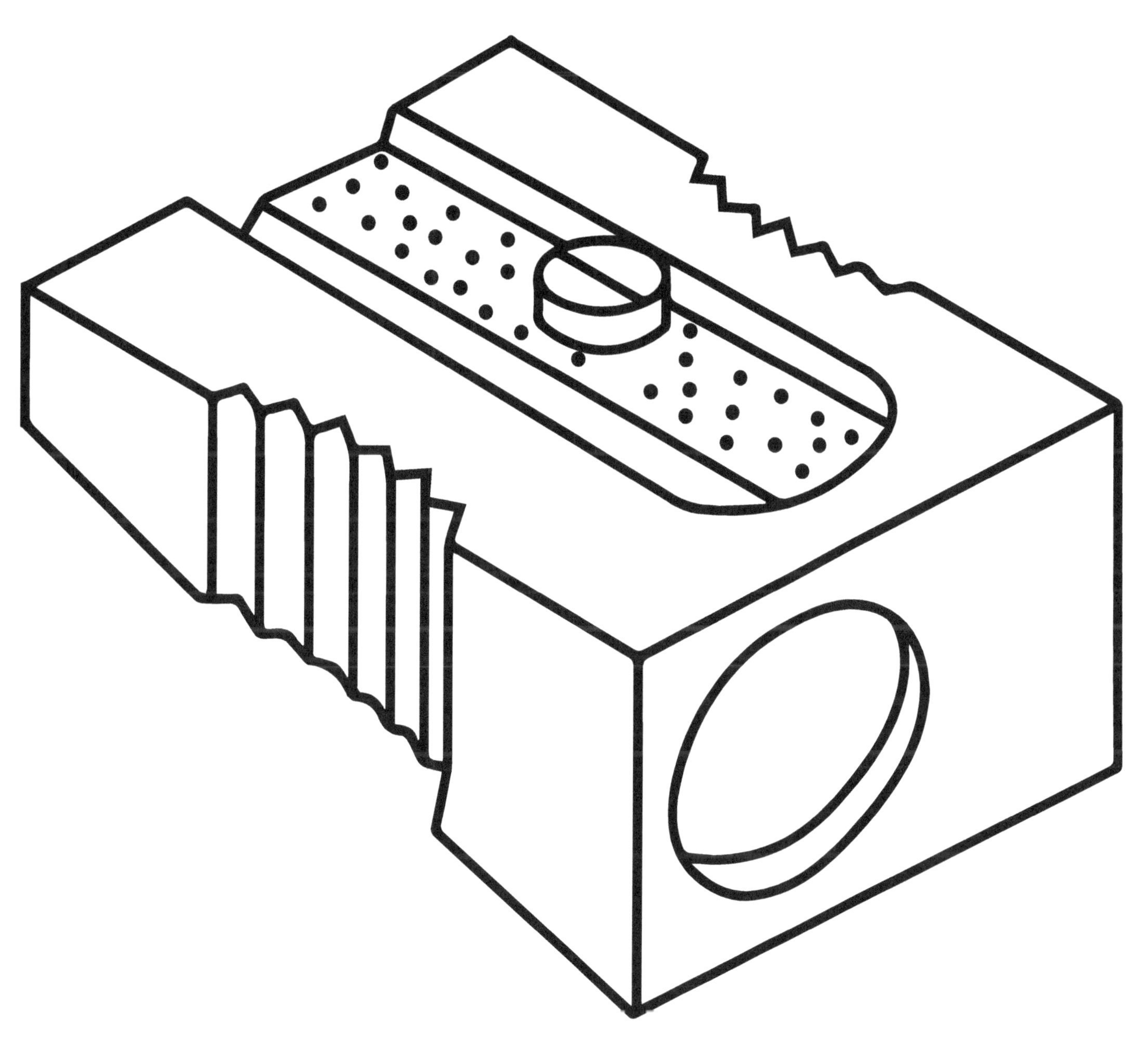